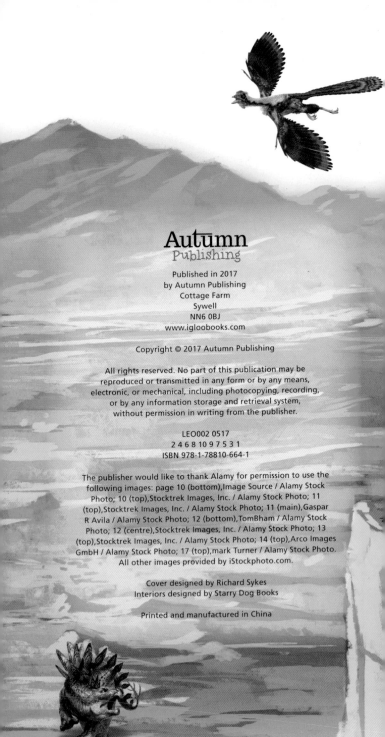

Autumn
Publishing

Published in 2017
by Autumn Publishing
Cottage Farm
Sywell
NN6 0BJ
www.igloobooks.com

LEO002 0517
2 4 6 8 10 9 7 5 3 1
ISBN 978-1-78810-664-1

The publisher would like to thank Alamy for permission to use the
following images: page 10 (bottom), Image Source / Alamy Stock
Photo; 10 (top), Stocktrek Images, Inc. / Alamy Stock Photo; 11
(top), Stocktrek Images, Inc. / Alamy Stock Photo; 11 (main), Gaspar
R Avila / Alamy Stock Photo; 12 (bottom), TomBham / Alamy Stock
Photo; 12 (centre), Stocktrek Images, Inc. / Alamy Stock Photo; 13
(top), Stocktrek Images, Inc. / Alamy Stock Photo; 14 (top), Arco Images
GmbH / Alamy Stock Photo; 17 (top), mark Turner / Alamy Stock Photo.
All other images provided by iStockphoto.com.

Cover designed by Richard Sykes
Interiors designed by Starry Dog Books

Printed and manufactured in China

OVER
100
FACTS FOR KIDS
DINOSAURS

Autumn
Publishing

The Prehistoric World

 FACT 1 Dinosaurs lived on Earth for more than 160 million years. Humans have only existed for 5 million years.

North America

Eurasia

South America

Africa

India

Australia

Antarctica

Pangaea

 FACT 2 The first dinosaurs appeared in the Triassic Period, 251–199 million years ago.

 FACT 3 In the Triassic Period, most of the world's land was squashed into one continent, Pangaea.

FACT 4 Pangaea had massive deserts. Huge storms and giant floods were common at this time.

FACT 5 The Jurassic Period (199–142 million years ago) came after the Triassic Period.

 FACT 6 Giant forests of fir trees grew across the Jurassic world.

Fir tree forest

The Jurassic Period

FACT 7 The Jurassic Period was the best time for dinosaurs and other other giant reptiles.

FACT 8 The last dinosaurs lived during the Cretaceous Period, 142–65 million years ago.

FACT 9 The first bees, ants and butterflies appeared in the Cretaceous Period.

FACT 10 The Cretaceous Period ended when a meteor struck Earth. This caused a change in climate that wiped out the dinosaurs.

Bees

Desert

What Were Dinosaurs?

FACT 11 Dinosaurs were reptiles that lived millions of years ago. They came in a wide range of shapes and sizes.

Stegosaurus   **Tyrannosaurus Rex**   **Brachiosaurus**

FACT 12 The word "dinosaur" means "terrible lizard". Dinosaurs got this name because the first fossils people found were very big.

FACT 13 Experts used to think that all dinosaurs had scaly skin, like lizards, but now they think some dinosaurs had feathers.

Ornitholestes

FACT 14 Dinosaurs lived alongside giant flying reptiles called pterosaurs, and huge swimming reptiles called plesiosaurs.

Pterosaur

FACT 15 The last dinosaurs died out 65 million years ago, about 60 million years before humans evolved.

FACT 16 Today's birds are descended from dinosaurs.

Flamingo

FACT 17 Everything we know about dinosaurs comes from looking at fossils (remains preserved in rock).

FACT 18 Some modern animals, such as crocodiles, are similar to prehistoric animals, but their ancestors were probably much bigger!

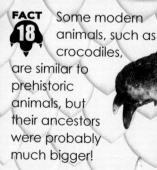
Crocodile

Giant
Predators

FACT 19 Dinosaurs included some of the biggest predators (animals that hunt other animals) ever to have lived.

Postosuchus

FACT 20 *Postosuchus* had hooked teeth for grabbing prey.

FACT 21 *Postosuchus* had long back legs but short front legs, suggesting it mostly walked on two feet.

FACT 22 *Allosaurus*, a fearsome Jurassic predator, had bony lumps over its eyes like small horns.

FACT 23 Some *Allosaurus* fossils have broken bones, probably from battling powerful prey such as *Stegosaurus*.

Allosaurus

FACT 24 *Spinosaurus* had long spines along its backbone that may have supported a large flap of skin.

Spinosaurus

FACT 25 *Spinosaurus* could swim as well as walk. Like a modern crocodile, it probably hunted both fish and land animals.

FACT 26 *Tyrannosaurus Rex* is thought to have had the most powerful bite of any creature in history.

FACT 27 *Tyrannosaurus* was about 12 m (40 ft) long (the length of a bus).

FACT 28 Another predator, *Giganotosaurus*, may have been even bigger. Only fragments of its skeleton have been found so far, so its size isn't known for certain.

Tyrannosaurus rex

11

Tiny Hunters

FACT 29 Theropods were dinosaurs that walked on two legs and mostly ate meat.

FACT 30 Some large theropods were hunters, but others were smaller and ate insects, reptiles, eggs and the remains of dead animals.

Caudipteryx

FACT 31 Many theropods probably had short feathers all over their bodies.

FACT 32 Some theropods, such as *Caudipteryx*, had beaks for crunching up fruit and shellfish.

FACT 33 *Coelophysis* lived in the Triassic Period. It had light, hollow bones and was a very fast runner.

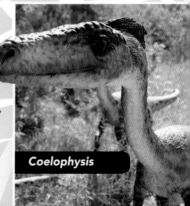

Coelophysis

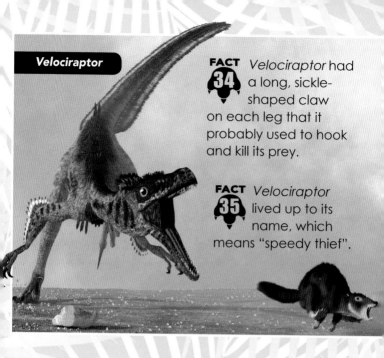

Velociraptor

FACT 34 *Velociraptor* had a long, sickle-shaped claw on each leg that it probably used to hook and kill its prey.

FACT 35 *Velociraptor* lived up to its name, which means "speedy thief".

FACT 36 *Microraptor* was one of the smallest dinosaurs. It only grew to about the size of a turkey.

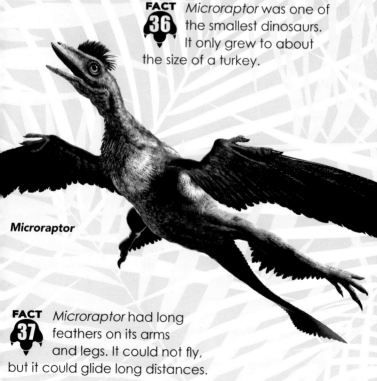

Microraptor

FACT 37 *Microraptor* had long feathers on its arms and legs. It could not fly, but it could glide long distances.

Plant Eaters

FACT 38 Plant-eating dinosaurs mostly walked on all fours and probably lived in herds.

FACT 39 *Pachycephalosaurus* had an extremely thick skull. Males may have competed by butting heads.

Pachycephalosaurus

Iguanodon

FACT 40 In the 1850s, people thought *Iguanodon* was a rhino-shaped dinosaur with a spike on its nose. Later they realised the spikes were on its thumbs.

FACT 41 *Iguanodon* was a large plant eater. It probably used its thumb spikes to defend itself.

Stegosaurus

FACT 42 *Stegosaurus*, or "roof lizard", got its name from the plates on its back that overlapped like roof tiles.

FACT 43 *Stegosaurus* may have used its plates to give out heat and keep itself cool.

FACT 44 Plant-eating *Triceratops* may have had up to 800 teeth in its jaws.

Triceratops

FACT 45 The bony ruff around *Triceratops'* neck may have been for protection, but more likely helped it to stay cool, like *Stegosaurus*'s plates.

Gentle Giants

FACT 46 Sauropods were the biggest kind of dinosaur. Their long necks could reach leaves at the very tops of trees.

Sauropod skull

FACT 47 Sauropods walked on four thick, strong legs, and had very long necks and tails.

FACT 48 Sauropods ate tough, stringy leaves, so their teeth wore out very quickly. They grew new ones every few weeks.

Sauropod tooth

Argentinosaurus

FACT 49 *Seismosaurus* is the longest dinosaur we know of. It grew up to 40 m (130 ft) long. That's as long as five buses.

Seismosaurus

FACT 50 *Diplodocus* was one of the first sauropods to be discovered.

FACT 51 *Sauroposeidon's* neck grew to 12 m (40 ft) long, making this dinosaur about three times the height of a giraffe.

FACT 52 New dinosaur fossils are being discovered every year. There may be even bigger species that we don't yet know about.

FACT 53 *Argentinosaurus* is the heaviest dinosaur ever discovered. It could have weighed up to 70 tonnes. That's as much as 12 large elephants.

17

Eggs
and Babies

Dinosaur egg

 FACT 54 Like modern birds, baby dinosaurs hatched out of eggs.

FACT 55 Dinosaur eggs often had rough, bumpy shells.

 FACT 56 The smallest dinosaur eggs were about 3 cm (1.2 in) long.

FACT 57 Some dinosaurs covered their eggs with leaves to keep them safe and warm.

FACT 58 Some dinosaurs, such as *Maiasaura* and *Compsognathus*, looked after their babies. Others left their babies to fend for themselves.

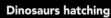

Dinosaurs hatching

FACT 59 *Diplodocus* eggs were about the size of ostrich eggs. This is very small given that *Diplodocus* was about 160 times bigger than an ostrich.

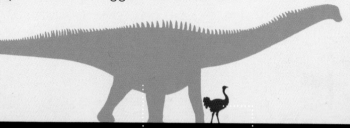

Diplodocus   **Ostrich**

FACT 60 Plant-eating dinosaurs mostly laid round eggs, like today's turtle eggs.

FACT 61 Theropods (two-legged, meat-eating dinosaurs) laid eggs shaped like modern birds' eggs.

Turtle eggs

FACT 62 Dinosaur babies were tiny compared to their parents. They had to be good at running and hiding until they could defend themselves.

Dinosaur Defences

FACT 63 Small dinosaurs and plant eaters had armour or weapons to defend themselves.

FACT 64 *Compsognathus* and other tiny dinosaurs had to rely on speed to escape from predators.

FACT 65 Small dinosaurs probably used camouflage to hide. However, we can't be sure, as fossils do not tell us what colour dinosaurs were.

Compsognathus

FACT 66 *Stegosaurus* had spikes up to 90 cm (36 in) long on the end of its tail.

FACT 67 Some experts believe sauropods used their tails like whips to beat off attackers.

Stegosaurus

20

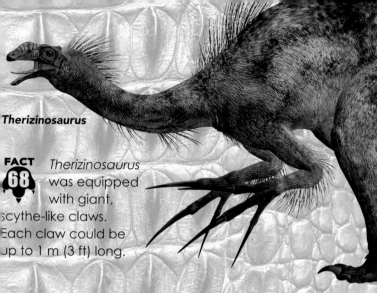

Therizinosaurus

FACT 68
Therizinosaurus was equipped with giant, scythe-like claws. Each claw could be up to 1 m (3 ft) long.

FACT 69
Therizinosaurus is one of the only known theropods (dinosaurs that walked on two legs) to eat plants instead of meat.

FACT 70
Weighing as much as three rhinos, *Ankylosaurus* was covered all over in thick armour.

FACT 71
As well as armour, *Ankylosaurus* had a heavy bone club on its tail to bash attackers.

Ankylosaurus

Flying Reptiles

FACT 72 Pterosaurs were giant, flying reptiles. They were not dinosaurs, but they lived at the same time.

FACT 73 Pterosaur wings were big flaps of skin that stretched between their ankles and their long front legs.

Pterosaur

FACT 74 Pterosaurs walked on four legs, folding their wings and using their front legs to support their weight.

FACT 75 Large pterosaurs hunted small land animals, grabbing them with their beaks as they walked along.

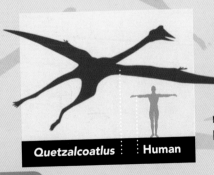

Quetzalcoatlus : Human

FACT 76 *Quetzalcoatlus* was one of the largest flying animals ever. Its wings stretched 10 m (33 ft), or more than five times the height of a human adult.

Pteranodon

FACT 77 *Pteranodons* lived by the sea and ate fish.

FACT 78 *Pteranodons* had large, bony crests on their skulls, probably used for attracting a partner.

Rhamphorhynchus

FACT 79 *Rhamphorhynchus* had a flap of skin at the end of its tail that it probably used to steer through the air.

FACT 80 *Archaeopteryx* was a dinosaur with feathers. It could fly, and was probably the ancestor of modern birds.

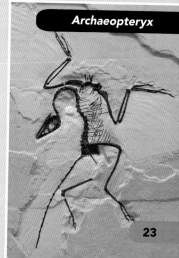

Archaeopteryx

Giant Swimmers

 FACT 81 The prehistoric oceans were home to some really enormous reptiles. They weren't dinosaurs or fish, but may have eaten both!

 FACT 82 *Ichthyosaurus* and its relatives were fish-shaped reptiles. They were expert at hunting underwater.

Ichthyosaurus

FACT 83 Long-necked *Plesiosaurus* and its relatives had flippers and lived underwater, but came to the surface to breathe.

 FACT 84 *Plesiosaurus* probably whipped its head from side to side to catch fish.

Plesiosaurus

FACT 85 *Nothosaurus* spent most of its time in the sea, grabbing fish with its long, sharp teeth.

FACT 86 *Nothosaurus* could also walk on land, and rested on the shore when it wasn't hunting.

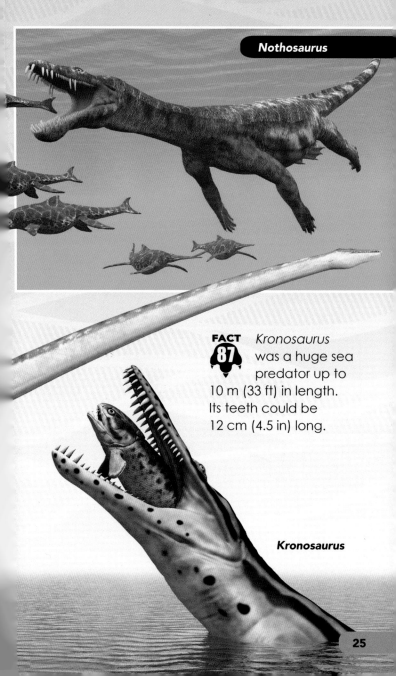

Nothosaurus

FACT 87 *Kronosaurus* was a huge sea predator up to 10 m (33 ft) in length. Its teeth could be 12 cm (4.5 in) long.

Kronosaurus

The End of the Dinosaurs

FACT 88 About 65 million years ago, almost every dinosaur species suddenly died out, along with the pterosaurs and giant sea reptiles.

Asteroid strike

FACT 89 Scientists believe a space rock or asteroid about 10 km (6 miles) wide crashed into Earth.

FACT 90 A crater more than 180 km (110 miles) across and 20 km (12 miles) deep can still be found where the asteroid landed.

FACT 91 When the asteroid hit, it sent up a cloud of dust that spread around the world, blocking out the sunlight.

Volcano

FACT 92 Giant volcanoes erupted about this time in what is now India, adding to the effects of the asteroid.

FACT 93 Earth became much cooler and plants died off. The dinosaurs died from cold and lack of food.

FACT 94 Up to three-quarters of the different types of animals on Earth died out completely.

Shrew

FACT 95 With the dinosaurs gone, birds and mammals became more common. Life on Earth began to look like it does today.

Fossils

 FACT 96 Fossils can form when animals or plants are buried in mud. Over time, their remains are replaced by minerals, which turn to stone.

Dinosaur fossil

FACT 97 The world's oldest fossils are 3,700 million years old. They show tiny bacteria that were some of the first life on Earth.

FACT 98 Fossils are very fragile, so most of the dinosaurs in museums are replicas.

Stegosaurus **skeleton**

 FACT 99 Most dinosaur fossils only include a few parts that scientists carefully piece together.

FACT 100 Fossils form in special, layered rocks called sedimentary rocks.

Sedimentary rock

Fossil fern

FACT 101 Plant fossils tell us that dinosaurs lived among fir trees and giant ferns.

FACT 102 Flowers only grew near to the end of the age of the dinosaurs.

Coproliths

FACT 103 Coproliths are fossils of dinosaur poo. They tell us what dinosaurs ate.

FACT 104 Fossil footprints tell us how dinosaurs walked and how fast they could run.

Fossil footprints